W9-AMN-819

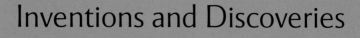

Inventions and Discoveries

Communication

WORLD BOOK

a Scott Fetzer company

Chicago

www.worldbookonline.com

World Book, Inc.
233 N. Michigan Avenue
Chicago, IL 60601
U.S.A.

For information about other World Book publications, visit
our Web site at **http://www.worldbookonline.com** or
call **1-800-WORLDBK (967-5325).**
For information about sales to schools and libraries, call
1-800-975-3250 (United States), or **1-800-837-5365
(Canada).**

Editorial:
Editor in Chief: Paul A. Kobasa
Project Managers: Cassie Mayer, Michael Noren
Editor: Jake Bumgardner
Content Development: Odyssey Books
Writer: Brad Davies
Researcher: Cheryl Graham
Manager, Contracts & Compliance
  (Rights & Permissions): Loranne K. Shields
Indexer: David Pofelski

Graphics and Design:
Associate Director: Sandra M. Dyrlund
Manager: Tom Evans
Coordinator, Design Development and Production:
  Brenda B. Tropinski
Designer: Matthew Carrington
Contributing Photographs Editor: Carol Parden
Senior Cartographer: John M. Rejba

Pre-Press and Manufacturing:
Director: Carma Fazio
Manufacturing Manager: Steven K. Hueppchen
Production/Technology Manager: Anne Fritzinger

Library of Congress Cataloging-in-Publication Data

Communication.
    p. cm. – (Inventions and discoveries)
  Includes index.
  Summary: "An exploration of the transformative impact of inventions and discoveries
in communication. Features include fact boxes, sidebars, biographies, and a timeline,
glossary, list of recommended reading and Web sites, and index"–Provided by publisher.
  ISBN 978-0-7166-0382-5
  1. Communication–Technological innovations–History–Juvenile literature.
I. World Book, Inc.
P96.T42C5985 2009
302.2–dc22
                            2008040648

Picture Acknowledgment:
Front Cover: © Vadim Ponomarenko, Alamy Images
Back Cover: Granger Collection

© Andrew Ammendolia, Alamy Images 39; © Corbis
Premium RF/Alamy Images 23; © Roger Cracknell
01/classic/Alamy Images 6; © dbimages/Alamy Images
37; © Digital Vision/Alamy Images 43; © David R. Frazier
Photolibrary/Alamy Images 15, 25; © Jeff Greenberg,
Alamy Images 33; © Steven Heald, Alamy Images 13;
©imagebroker/Alamy Images 40; © vikki martin, Alamy
Images 7; © mm-images/Alamy Images 43; Otis
Images/Alamy Images 5; © Photo Researchers/Alamy
Images 29; © Photodisc/Alamy Images 21; © Vadim
Ponomarenko, Alamy Images 35; © Print Collector/Alamy
Images 20; © shinypix/Alamy Images 38; © Hugh
Threlfall, Alamy Images 42; © Travelshots.com/Alamy
Images 23; © vario images GmbH & Co./Alamy Images
41; AP Wide World Photos 31, 34; © Alinari/Art Resource
8; © Werner Forman, Art Resource 4, 10; © Erich Lessing,
Art Resource 8,9; The Metropolitan Museum of Art/Art
Resource 7; The New York Public Library/Art Resource
17; © Snark, Art Resource 13; © Bettmann/Corbis 16, 27,
29, 32; © The British Library, London 12; © Time & Life
Pictures/Getty Images 31; Granger Collection 14,15, 18,
19, 22, 24. 25, 28; Lewis Hine/Library of Congress 26;
© Peter Bowater, Photo Researchers 11; Shutterstock 5,
31, 38, 44

All maps and illustrations are the exclusive property of
World Book, Inc.

Inventions and Discoveries
Set ISBN: 978-0-7166-0380-1
Printed in China
1 2 3 4 5 12 11 10 09

► Table of Contents

There is a glossary of terms on pages 45-46. Terms defined in the glossary are in type **that looks like this** on their first appearance on any spread (two facing pages).

► Introduction

What is an invention?

An invention is a new device, new product, or new way of doing something. Inventions change the way we live. Before the car was invented, some people rode horses to travel long distances. Before the light bulb was invented, people used candles and similar sources of light to see at night. The invention of farming methods allowed people to stay in one place instead of wandering in search of food. As people established villages and invented ways to travel to other villages, trade (the exchange of goods) flourished. Technological advances soon produced a great variety of new goods, services, and capabilities. Today, inventions continue to shape people's lives every day.

Early inventions like the horse-drawn chariot (cart) would dramatically change people's lives.

Wireless Internet allows people to communicate in many different ways from nearly anywhere on the planet.

What is communication?

Communication is the sharing of ideas and information. People can share information through spoken and written words, by making and looking at images, and by making and listening to sounds. People can also communicate through gestures and facial expressions.

Over time, people have developed ways to share information with many people at once. Such methods of **mass communication** have included books, magazines, newspapers, **television,** radio, and, more recently, the **Internet.** Communication also takes place through sound recordings, motion pictures, and signs. Taken together, these tools allow people all over the world to communicate with one another.

Cellular telephones can be used in nearly every corner of the world.

► Language and Writing

No one knows exactly how or when language was invented. The first words could have been spoken many thousands or even millions of years ago. Language slowly developed as a system of signals used to communicate. These signals included sounds and hand signs, which later became words and letters. Language gave people the ability to speak to one another and to record their thoughts and ideas.

From those first spoken words came stories and histories. People wanted to understand themselves and the world around them. To do so, they created **legends** and **myths.** They passed along these stories through word of mouth. The stories were then passed on from generation to generation.

Ancient Neandertals drew pictures of bison and many other animals on cave walls throughout what is now France.

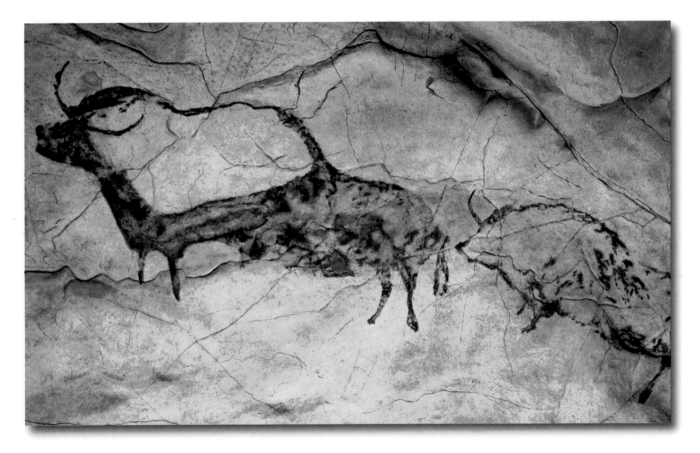

Deaf and hearing-impaired people use sign language to communicate. Sign language uses hand signals, body language, and facial expressions instead of sound. A French educator named Laurent Clerc introduced sign language to deaf people in the United States in the early 1800's. He helped set up the American School for the Deaf, which opened in Hartford, Connecticut, in 1817.

Writing began to develop when people started drawing pictures to represent things. People drew pictures of animals and themselves. Later, they drew pictures to represent ideas. For example, they drew smiling faces to represent happiness. These symbols expressed feelings that we still understand today.

The first real writing began about 5,500 years ago (3500 B.C.). Middle Eastern people called the Sumerians made the first picture writing. They created symbols to stand for the words of their own language. They wrote these symbols on clay tablets, recording things like prayers and laws. They also recorded thoughts on science, mathematics, and medicine.

This clay tablet shows an early form of writing. The tablet dates back to 3000 B.C.

▶ The Alphabet

The Ancient Egyptians used hieroglyphic writing to record their histories and legends.

People of the ancient world eventually developed **alphabets,** in which symbols stood for particular sounds instead of words. With alphabets, fewer symbols were needed for writing, because it was not necessary to have a symbol for each word in the language. The same symbols could be combined in different ways to make different words.

About 5,000 years ago (3000 B.C.), the Egyptians, in northeastern Africa, developed a system of writing called **hieroglyphics** (*HY uhr uh GLIHF ihks*). Like Sumerian writing, hieroglyphics used pictures to repre-

sent words. Hieroglyphic writing also included symbols for **syllables** (separate sounds that make up words).

About 3,500 years ago (1500 B.C.), Middle Eastern people called the Semites developed their own alphabet based on the Egyptian system. They used some of the pictures from Egyptian hieroglyphics, but they used these symbols for sounds in their own language.

Five hundred years later (around 1000 B.C.), the Phoenicians (*fuh NIHSH uhns*), who lived along the coast of the Mediterranean Sea, developed an alphabet of 22 signs. This alphabet was related to the Semitic alphabet and Egyptian hieroglyphics.

Phoenician writing was advanced for its day, but it had no signs for vowels.

The first known writing systems and alphabets were developed in the Middle East.

Sometime before 800 B.C., people in Greece came into contact with Phoenician traders. Through this contact, the Greeks learned the idea of writing individual sounds of language. They borrowed the Phoenician symbols and changed them to make the Greek alphabet. They also added signs for **vowel** sounds, which could be combined with **consonants** to spell any word they wanted.

The Greeks also adopted the Phoenician names for their signs. The first letter, called *aleph* in Phoenician, became *alpha* in Greek. The second letter, *beth*, became *beta* in Greek. The word *alphabet* comes from the names of these first two letters in the Greek alphabet, *alpha* and *beta*.

The ancient **Romans** made their own letters, influenced heavily by the Greek alphabet. The Roman letters looked much the same as the letters used today in the English alphabet and other languages.

Many other systems of writing developed from the Phoenician system. Examples include the Arabic and Hebrew alphabets, as well as some alphabets that are used in different parts of India.

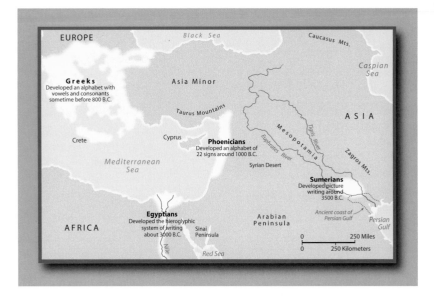

The Greeks added vowels to their alphabet but they didn't put spaces between words.

The Roman, or Latin, alphabet was very similar to our own, but Romans wrote only in capital letters.

► Paper

This is a page from a book that was printed in China in A.D. 868.

This is an illustration on papyrus from an ancient Egyptian book.

Long ago, people wrote on stones, clay, animal skins, and even bones to communicate their ideas. In ancient Egypt, people made paper by cutting thin strips from the **papyrus** (*puh PY ruhs*) plant. They crisscrossed the strips and pressed them together, creating a sheet of material they could write on. The word *paper* comes from the word *papyrus*.

The kind of paper we use today was developed in China. People there started making paper more than 2,000 years ago (about 300 B.C.). At first, they used fibers (threadlike pieces) from the hemp plant or the bark of the mulberry tree. Later, they used fibers from rags, rope, and fishing nets. The first Chinese paper was used for wrapping objects and as clothing, but it was too rough to be written on. The Chinese style of papermaking soon spread to countries in the Middle East and Europe.

When European settlers came to America, they brought the art of papermaking with them. The first paper **mill** in America was built near Philadelphia, Pennsylvania, in 1690. At first, these mills used rags to make paper. But a rag shortage forced people to look for a new material. By the 1800's, people began making paper from wood pulp (ground-up wood).

A CLOSER LOOK

The ancient Alexandrian Library needed nearly all the papyrus available in Egypt to stock its shelves with scrolls, or rolled strips of paper. As a result, parchment, a type of paper made from animal skin, became popular elsewhere. Parchment was widely used until modern paper replaced it in the **Middle Ages.**

Today, more than 390 million tons (355 million metric tons) of paper is made each year. The United States is the leading paper-producing country.

Giant rollers and presses do most of the work in a modern paper mill.

▶ Movable Type

With the invention of paper, people could share their ideas and record history through written text. But to share these ideas widely, they had to write out copies of the text by hand. People soon began to think of ways to speed the process of copying written words.

By A.D. 700, the Chinese, Japanese, and Koreans had developed **block printing.** This process involved carving groups of symbols and pictures onto wood blocks, putting ink on the raised images, and pressing the inked block onto paper. Block printing spread to countries in Europe in the late 1300's.

About 1045, a Chinese printer named Bi Sheng made the first **movable type** out of clay blocks. Instead of putting groups of symbols together on a single block, Bi Sheng used a separate block for each Chinese symbol or character. These carved blocks could

These pages were printed in Korea using bronze movable type in 1434.

be used over and over again. After printing a page, a printer could simply separate the pieces of type and re-arrange them to create a new text.

Because the Chinese language has many different characters, Bi Sheng's method of printing was not very practical and eventually fell out of use. However, movable type would become extremely important in Europe about 400 years later.

Before movable type was invented, people had to write each letter by hand. The Book of Kells, above, was written in Ireland between the mid-700's and early 800's.

These type pieces were used in Europe around the mid-1800's.

▶ The Printing Press

This English engraving shows a steam-driven printing press from 1826.

Between 1300 and 1600, a cultural movement called the **Renaissance** (rebirth) swept across Europe. The Renaissance was a period of great advancement in educational and artistic ideas, and it created a huge demand for books. Hand copying and **block printing** could not keep up with this demand.

In about 1440, a German inventor named Johannes (*YOH HAHN UHS*) Gutenberg developed a **print-ing press** that used **movable type.** His machine was based on the design of a wine press, a machine that people used to press the juice from grapes to make wine. Gutenberg made separate pieces of metal type for each letter of the **alphabet.** He assembled the pieces in a frame to form pages and applied ink to the type. The machine pressed the inked type against paper to print words.

The Gutenberg press could print about 300 copies of a page daily. By 1500, there were more than 1,000 print shops in Europe, and several million books had been produced.

Many people called the new method of printing a "black art," because they feared it was evil. They could not understand how books could be produced so quickly, or how all copies could look exactly alike. Despite people's fears, printing quickly became an important communication tool. It significantly increased the production of religious texts. In addition, debates about social problems, religious beliefs, and government matters quickly appeared in print.

Johannes Gutenberg

Johannes Gutenberg was born in Mainz, Germany, sometime around 1395. Because of his family's involvement in a disagreement in his home community, Gutenberg had to spend several years in Strasbourg, France. There, he carried on experiments to develop a method for printing books that would replace hand copying. He came up with practical ways to use movable metallic type for printing. By 1440, he had invented the printing press.

There were few changes to the printing press from Gutenberg's time until the 1800's. In 1811, a German named Friedrich König invented a steam-powered press that could print about 1,100 sheets per hour. In 1846, Richard Hoe of the United States invented a press that used rotating cylinders (revolving drums) to print 8,000 sheets per hour. Later models turned out as many as 20,000 sheets per hour.

The printing press is one of the most important inventions in history. It has enabled millions of people to receive knowledge through books, newspapers, magazines, and other printed formats.

Newspapers are printed by the thousands, like these copies of the *Houston Chronicle*.

▶ Lithography

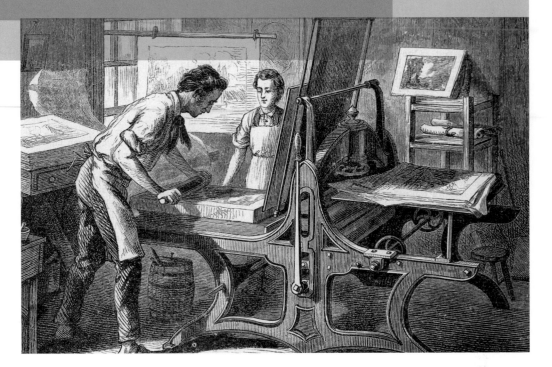

A master shows his apprentice the art of lithography.

In 1798, a young German writer named Alois Senefelder (*AH loys ZAY nuh FEHL duhr*) came up with a new way to print words onto paper. He wanted to make copies of a play he had written, and he was preparing to **etch** a stone slab for printing. He wrote on the slab with a wax crayon and found that the marks could be inked and printed. With this discovery, Senefelder invented a new printing process called **lithography.**

Lithography is based on the principle that water does not mix with grease. An artist can use a grease pencil, a crayon, or a greasy liquid called tusche (*TUSH uh*) to draw a picture on a flat surface, such as limestone rock, or a specially prepared plate. After the picture is drawn, the artist wets the surface with water. The water sticks only to the parts that are not covered by the greasy design.

Next, the artist uses a roller to apply an oil-based ink to the surface. The ink sticks only to the greasy areas but not to the wet areas. In the final step, the artist places a sheet of paper on the printing surface and places it into a **printing press** to transfer the inked design onto paper.

Soon after Senefelder invented lithography, European artists began using the method creatively. The early masters of lithography included the French artists Eugene Delacroix (*oo ZHEHN duh lah KRWAH*) and Honore Daumier (*aw naw RAY doh MYAY*). During the late 1800's, French painters, such as Henri de Toulouse-Lautrec (*ahn REE duh too LOOZ loh TREHK*) used lithography to create masterpieces. Leading lithographers of the 1900's included Marc Chagall (*shah GAHL*) and Pablo Picasso in Europe and Jasper Johns and Joseph Pennell in the United States.

Today, metal plates have replaced Senefelder's stone, and images are placed on the plates and transferred to paper with more advanced techniques. The process is used for such mass-produced items as books, cards, magazines, stationery, cans, cartons, labels, and newspapers. In fact, most printing today is done by lithography.

A lithographer draws with a greasy crayon, applies water and ink, and presses paper to make a print.

Henri de Toulouse-Lautrec became famous for his lithographic posters advertising the Moulin Rouge cabaret club in Paris, France.

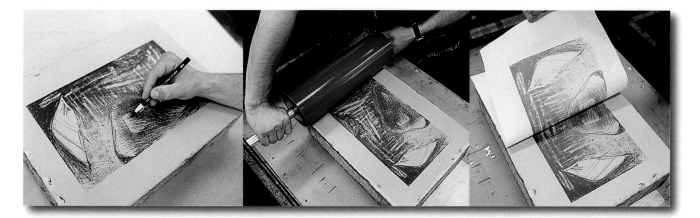

▶ The Telegraph

The telegraph was an important means of communication from the mid-1800's to the mid-1900's.

B y the mid-1800's, people could share ideas through books, newspapers, and other written texts. However, there was still no way for people to communicate quickly if they were located in two different places. This would begin to change with the arrival of the electric **telegraph,** which could send messages by using **electric current** traveling along wires.

In 1820, a Danish scientist named Hans Christian Oersted (*UR stehd*) found that an electric current can cause a magnetized needle to move. This discovery led to the invention of the telegraph. In communication by telegraph, an operator would send a message by using a special device to vary the electric current flowing through the wires. When the amount of electricity changed, a device at the receiving end would convert the signals into a specific series of clicks. An operator would then decode these clicks into words, or a **telegram.**

A number of inventors created early telegraphic devices. In 1830, an American named Joseph Henry set up a simple telegraph using **electromagnets.** Electromagnets are pieces of soft iron that become strong magnets when wrapped in a wire carrying an electric current. Henry's device sent signals over more than 1 mile (1.6 kilometers) of wire.

In England, William Cooke and Charles Wheatstone invented a device using electromagnets and needles. Their telegraph sent messages using five needles connected to separate wires. Pulses of electric current caused two needles at a time to move and point to individual letters. Cooke and Wheatstone **patented** their telegraph in England in 1837. They continued work on it after that date.

The American painter and inventor Samuel F. B. Morse is credited with making the first practical telegraph in 1837. Morse received a U.S. patent for it in 1840. However, Morse's invention built upon years of research and experiments by people who came before him.

The telegraph became an important way to send information quickly to different locations. Reporters used the telegraph to send stories to their newspapers. Armies on both sides of the American Civil War (1861-1865) also relied heavily on the invention. The number of telegrams sent in the United States reached its peak in 1929, when more than 200 million were **transmitted.**

Samuel F.B. Morse

Samuel F. B. Morse was born on April 27, 1791, in Massachusetts. He received the patent for the first successful electric telegraph in the United States in 1840. He also invented Morse code, a system of sending messages using short and long sounds combined in various ways.

Though Morse was a famous inventor, his real passion was art. He studied painting and sculpture in Europe and later found fame as a portrait painter. Morse also helped start the National Academy of Design and served as its first president.

The Fax Machine

This early version of a fax machine dates back to 1896. It would take nearly 100 years before faxes were practical enough for everyday use.

This faxed image of a boy and his dog was produced from the original picture in 1896.

During the 1800's, the **Industrial Revolution** introduced power-driven machinery and factories that led to the swift production of large amounts of goods. Improved transportation methods meant that these goods could be shipped more easily and quickly than before to different parts of the world. Fast, long-distance communication became more important than ever.

In 1842, a Scottish scientist and clockmaker named Alexander Bain came up with a new communication

device that came to be called the **fax machine.** The word *fax* comes from the Latin word *facsimile* (*fak SIHM uh lee*), which means "exact copy." Today, fax machines can send and receive written words and images over **telephone** lines.

The first fax system was expensive and difficult to work, so it did not become popular or practical for quite some time. Even so, many inventors in Europe and the United States worked hard to improve the devices. By the 1930's, news companies were using fax machines to send photographs. By the 1980's, fax machines had finally become everyday office features.

For a fax system to work, both the sender and the receiver must have a fax machine. The sender puts a document into the machine and dials the number of the fax machine to which the document is being sent.

Once a telephone connection is made, the sending machine scans (reads) the document to make an electric signal that matches the light and dark spots of the document. The receiving machine uses the signal to produce an exact copy of the document.

The development of the fax machine enabled people throughout the world to exchange documents and other printed materials in only minutes. During the late 1900's, fax machines became an essential tool for a wide range of businesses.

Modern fax machines are found in offices and homes around the world.

▶ The Typewriter

The Sholes & Glidden Type Writer was produced by E. Remington & Sons in New York beginning in 1874.

Though the **fax machine** was invented 25 years before the **typewriter,** the *click-clack* of typewriters was heard in offices long before the fax machine became widely used. For most of the 1900's, nearly every business document, magazine story and newspaper article had to first be typed on a typewriter.

In 1867, Christopher Latham Sholes, an inventor from Milwaukee, Wisconsin, designed the first practical typewriter with the help of Carlos Glidden and Samuel W. Soule. To type a letter or number on a typewriter, a person would simply press a key that was labeled with that letter or number. When pressed down, the key caused a metal bar to swing up and strike an inked ribbon that rested in front of a piece of paper. The end of the bar had the shape of the letter or number on it. The force of the bar hitting the ribbon transferred the image of the letter or number onto the paper.

The earliest typewriters had letters arranged alphabetically so that a typist could easily locate keys. However, when a typist struck, one right after the other, two or more keys whose type bars were next to one another, the bars frequently jammed. To fix this problem, Sholes helped develop a keyboard where the most commonly

The QWERTY keyboard is the most widely used keyboard for computers and typewriters.

typed letters were spaced apart. The new design became known as the QWERTY keyboard, named after the letters that appear near the keyboard's upper-left corner. The QWERTY keyboard appeared in 1874 and is still used for keyboards in most English-speaking countries.

With the earliest typewriters, pressing down on the keys required some effort from the typist to move the bars with sufficient force to transfer ink to paper. The electric typewriter, which came into use in the 1920's, required less effort because an electric motor provided the needed force. In the 1970's, **electronic** typewriters were invented. These contained a computer chip that could store information and allow certain functions to be completed automatically. By 1980, **personal computers** and printers started to replace typewriters for home and office use.

The Telephone

For most of the 1800's, there was no way for people at two distant locations to speak to each other directly. They could communicate only by sending letters or **telegrams.** But in the 1870's, a Scottish-born inventor named Alexander Graham Bell discovered a way to send people's voices across long distances.

In 1871, Bell arrived in Boston, Massachusetts, to become a teacher to people who were deaf. He performed experiments at night, working to improve the **telegraph** by creating a device that could send several telegraph messages over one wire at the same time.

On June 2, 1875, while conducting an experiment, Bell had a break-

Bell's telephone is shown here in illustrations from an English newspaper in 1877.

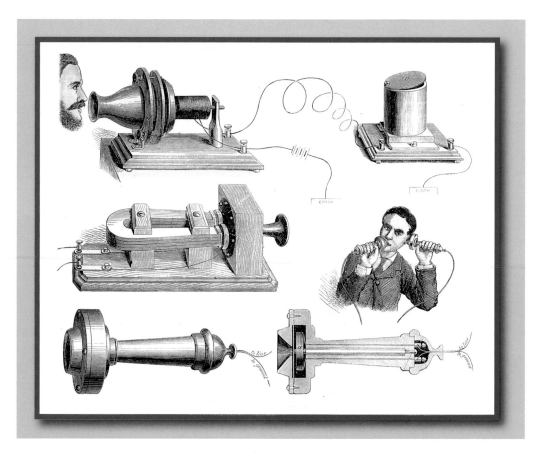

Alexander Graham Bell

Alexander Graham Bell (1847-1922) was born in Edinburgh, Scotland. His mother was a painter, and his father helped teach people who were deaf to speak. Bell also was an educator of deaf students, but he is best known as the inventor of the telephone.

Bell and his assistant, Thomas Watson, helped start telephone service in the United States. In 1877, Bell married Mabel Hubbard, one of his students, and they took the invention to England. But Bell did not stay in the telephone business. Instead, he preferred to continue his work with the deaf and to develop other inventions. Bell became a U.S. citizen in 1882.

through. One of the metal reeds (thin pieces) on his device got stuck. Bell's assistant, Thomas Watson, plucked the reed to loosen it. In the other room, Bell heard the sound in his receiver. He realized that the vibrating reed had created changes to the **electric current** that passed through the wire. These changes were then reproduced in the receiver at the other end of the wire.

This discovery led to more experiments, and Bell received a **patent** for the first **telephone** on March 7, 1876. Three days later, he **transmitted** human speech over a telephone for the first time. In 1877, the Bell Telephone Company was founded. Within 10 years, there were more than 150,000 people who owned telephones in the United States.

Today, most people take the telephone for granted. With a worldwide network of telephone wires, it is easy for people to call someone in a different part of the world.

People at home and at work rely every day on communicating by phone.

A young boy sells newspapers on the street in Wilmington, Delaware, in 1910.

Before radio, **television,** and the **Internet,** newspapers provided the best way for important information to reach many people. By 1830, newspapers were published almost everywhere in the world.

Up until the 1880's, printers arranged individual metal letters into words and paragraphs to print a page and then rearranged the letters for each new page. But in 1884, a German-born clockmaker named Ottmar Mergenthaler **patented** a printing machine called the **Linotype,** which could produce an entire "line of type" at once.

On the Linotype, a person types a line of text into a keyboard that drives the machine to arrange tiny brass molds for the letters of the line of text. When a line of text is complete, the operator presses a key that causes molten (melted) metal to be sent into a tray with the line of brass molds. When the metal cools, it hardens into a single line of type called a slug. When all the lines for a single page are prepared, they are inked and printed. After printing, the slugs are melted down so that the metal can be used again.

The *New York Tribune* gave the Linotype its first major commercial use in 1886. In 1890, Mergenthaler introduced an improved machine called the Simplex Linotype, which became a worldwide success.

The Linotype significantly im-proved the speed of **typesetting** (the process of preparing type for printing). It also reduced the cost of printing. This allowed newspapers to be sold more cheaply, so more peo-ple could now afford to buy them.

Linotype machines were used in nearly all typesetting work until the 1960's. Today, newer typesetting methods, such as **photocomposition** and computer typesetting, have be-come more common in the United States and many other countries.

A typesetter works at the keyboard of the Linotype ma-chine in the 1900's.

▶ Radio

The **telegraph** and the **telephone** enabled people at distant locations to communicate with each other, but only if the locations were connected by wires. This began to change in the late 1800's, when scientists discovered ways to send **radio signals** through the air. The invention of the radio allowed people to communicate quickly between any two points on land, at sea,

Guglielmo Marconi poses with his wireless radio receiver in 1896.

and, later, in the sky and in space.

The development of the radio began in the 1830's with an idea proposed separately by an American professor named Joseph Henry and a British scientist named Michael Faraday. Both Henry and Faraday proposed that an **electric current** in one wire could produce an electric current in another wire, even when the wires are not connected. Another British scientist, James Maxwell, explained this idea by suggesting that **electromagnetic waves** travel through the air. Electromagnetic waves are related patterns of electric and magnetic force that are created by the back-and-forth movement of electric charges. In the late 1880's, the German scientist Heinrich Hertz (*HYN rihkh hehrts*) performed experiments that proved Maxwell's theory of electromagnetic waves.

Though many people contributed to the radio's development, Nikola Tesla, an American inventor from Austria Hungary, is credited with its invention. In 1891, he invented the Tesla coil, an extremely important component (part) of radio **transmitters.**

In 1895, an Italian inventor named Guglielmo Marconi (*goo LYEHL moh mahr KOH nee*) sent radio signals more than a mile through the air in the form of telegraph code signals. In 1901, Marconi's equipment **transmitted** signals all the way across the Atlantic Ocean, from England to Canada. In 1906, a Canadian-born scientist named Reginald Fessenden first transmitted voice by radio.

Radio **broadcasting** (programming) began on a large scale during the 1920's. Soon, families could gather in their living rooms to listen to comedies, adventure dramas, live music, variety shows, and other kinds of radio programming.

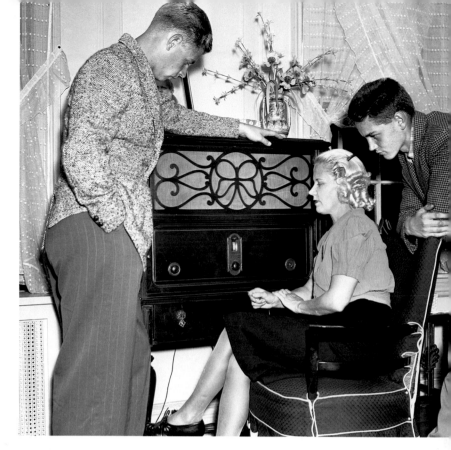

Families used to gather around the radio to listen to news, sports, and entertainment.

Nikola Tesla

Nikola Tesla (1856-1943) was born in Austria Hungary, in an area that is now part of Croatia. In 1884, Tesla left Europe for the United States. He worked for the inventor Thomas Edison but quit after one year.

Tesla became a pioneer in electrical technology, and he received more than 100 **patents** for a variety of inventions. His Tesla coil is still used in radio and **television** transmission today. Tesla's other achievements include groundbreaking work with **X rays**, radar, aircraft design, and neon and fluorescent lighting.

► Television

By the early 1900's, when operators were first **transmitting** words by radio, many scientists had begun experimenting with the transmission of pictures. These experiments eventually led to the development of the **television**—a tremendously popular communication system that is used daily in nearly every corner of the world.

Many scientists contributed to the invention of television. Among them was Philo Farnsworth, an American scientist who created an **electronic** scanning system in 1922. This became a breakthrough in television technology. In 1929, a Russian-born American scientist named Vladimir Zworykin demonstrated the first practical, completely electronic television system.

A CLOSER LOOK

Ways Television Signals Reach Homes

(1) **Satellites** beam television signals to satellite dishes mounted outside homes.

(2) Antennas on roofs or TV sets receive signals from local television stations.

(3) Cable television signals are sent to homes through an underground cable.

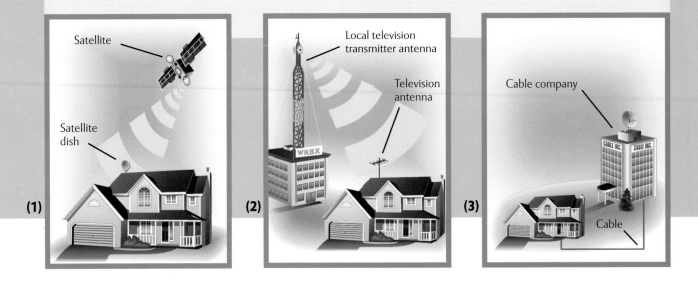

(1) Satellite / Satellite dish

(2) Local television transmitter antenna / Television antenna / WKBX

(3) Cable company / CABLE INC. / Cable

The 1960 United States presidential debates between John F. Kennedy and Richard M. Nixon demonstrated the power of television.

Television works by changing pictures and sounds into electronic signals, which are then sent through the air. A television set receives these signals and turns them back into pictures and sounds.

The first television **broadcast,** by the British Broadcasting Corporation (BBC) in the United Kingdom, occurred in 1936. In 1939, the National Broadcasting Company (NBC) became the first company to broadcast television in the United States. However, television had limited impact until the late 1940's, when stations, or transmitting locations, began sending program signals from a **transmitter** over the air to **antennas** in homes.

As more families came to own television sets, TV programming began to influence people's attitudes and beliefs. By watching TV shows, viewers can see the latest fashions and hear the opinions of people with different backgrounds and beliefs. Through advertisements, people are encouraged to buy certain products. Television also plays a major role in how people learn about their government and select their leaders.

► The Handheld Radio

After the invention of the radio, people began to design smaller radios that could both **transmit** and receive messages, allowing for two-way communication. The first portable two-way radios required the user to wear a backpack that was connected to a large handheld receiver. These backpack models and smaller handheld models proved to be very important for military forces during World War II (1939-1945).

As technology advanced, portable two-way radios, commonly known as **walkie-talkies,** became more widely used. Walkie-talkies include handheld models and **citizens band (CB)** radios. Most handheld models can transmit and receive any of 14

The walkie-talkies used by these American soldiers in 1945 are larger than modern two-way radios.

channels. Handheld radios can send their signals over distances of about 2 miles (3.2 kilometers), though their range depends on what obstacles (such as trees, hills, and buildings) stand in the way. Cheaper handheld models are sometimes sold as toys. These models generally operate on only one channel and have a smaller range. CB radios can transmit and receive any of 40 channels. They can transmit up to about 4 miles (6.4 kilometers).

Police, firefighters, construction workers, and others rely on walkie-talkies for quick voice communication. Some types of walkie-talkies require a special license to operate.

FUN FACT

The backpack walkie-talkies used during World War II were quite heavy. They weighed about 40 pounds (18 kilograms) but had a range of 10 to 20 miles (16 to 32 kilometers). The smaller handheld units weighed just 5 pounds (2.3 kilograms) but only worked over distances of 1 to 3 miles (1.6 to 4.8 kilometers).

► The Satellite

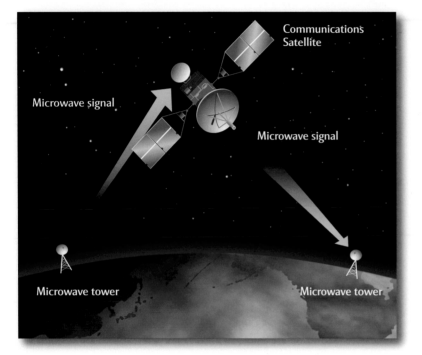

Communications satellites act as message relays as they orbit Earth.

An **artificial satellite** (*SAT uh lyt*) is a human-made object that orbits (moves around) an object in space. A communications satellite is a type of artificial satellite that receives radio, **television,** and other signals in space and relays (sends) them back to Earth.

Interestingly, a British science-fiction writer named Arthur C. Clarke is credited with inventing communi-

cations satellites. In an article published in 1945, Clarke described a satellite in orbit that could serve as an information relay station in the sky. This idea would turn out to be one of the greatest advances in modern communication.

Because a satellite is high above Earth, it can direct radio waves to any location within a large region. Without satellites, most radio transmissions could not reach far beyond the horizon (the distant, curved line where the land and sky appear to

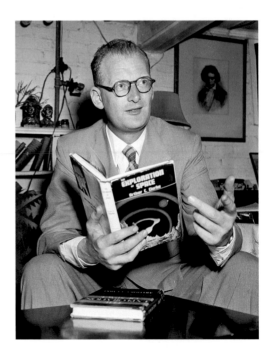

Arthur C. Clarke reads from his book, *The Exploration of Space*, in 1952.

meet). Satellites can send messages to many places at once, and they offer instant service when radio links are needed quickly.

The United States launched the first communications satellite, named Score, on December 18, 1958. It **broadcast** a taped greeting from President Dwight D. Eisenhower. Another satellite, named Echo 1, was launched on August 12, 1960. It was the first satellite to relay voice messages from one location to another.

Early communications satellites were built to carry long-distance **telephone** calls. Satellites still perform this task today, providing service in places where it is difficult to install telephone cables. Satellites also send telephone signals across oceans and to people in remote places. A ship's crew at sea, for instance, can talk to people anywhere in the world on mobile satellite phones.

Today, communications satellites also play a major role in television **broadcasting.** Satellites deliver programs to local cable TV companies or directly to homes. Satellite TV subscribers use dish-shaped **antennas** to receive hundreds of TV **channels.**

These large satellite dishes send and receive signals to and from space.

The Internet

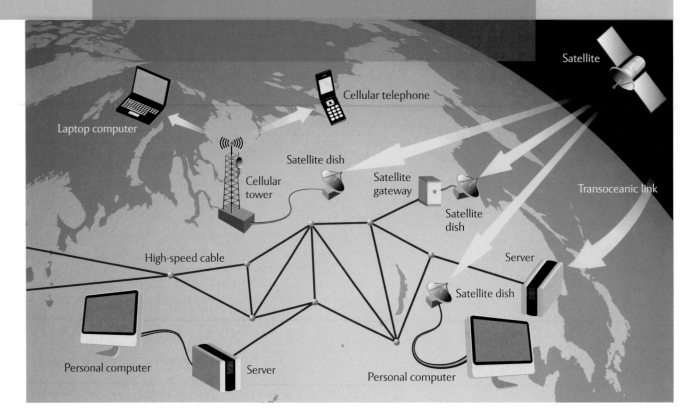

Labels within image: Satellite · Cellular telephone · Laptop computer · Satellite dish · Satellite gateway · Cellular tower · Satellite dish · Transoceanic link · Satellite dish · High-speed cable · Server · Server · Personal computer · Personal computer

High-speed cables, cellular towers, and satellites can be used to connect a computer to the Internet.

Computers first came into practical use in the mid-1900's. However, for many years, there was no way to link computers together to allow the sharing of information among them. Over the second half of the 1900's, the emergence of the **Internet** became one of the most important breakthroughs in the history of communication.

In the 1960's, the United States government's Department of Defense developed a network (interconnected system) of military and government computers. The network was intended to protect the information on those computers in case of a war or disaster. Soon, universities, corporations, and other organizations developed their own computer networks. Eventually, these networks joined with the government network to form the Internet. The word *Internet* means an interconnected network of networks.

The wider application, or use, of the Internet began in 1991. That year, a British computer scientist named Tim Berners-Lee developed the **World Wide Web.** The Web is made up of **electronic** addresses called Web sites, which contain Web pages that hold information. People can use the Web to access, or get to, an enormous range of documents, illustrations, sounds, and moving pictures. In many ways, the Web resembles a vast library of interconnected information. Programs called **search engines** help people sort through this huge amount of information to find what they want.

The Internet enables users of computers and similar devices to send and receive messages called **e-mail,** or electronic mail. Many people communicate over the Internet using **instant messaging (IM).** This feature enables two people to communicate through text messages that can be

seen by both users as the messages are typed. People can also see and speak to one another through microphones and cameras that are connected to the Internet.

New technologies continue to change the way people use the Internet. Handheld computers and special types of **cellular telephones** enable users to access the Internet from almost any location.

Internet cafes, like this one in China, are popular around the world.

▶ The Cellular Telephone

This 1991 Motorola mobile phone is already considered a bulky antique.

Cell phones are an important business and personal communication tool for many people.

Cellular telephones, commonly called mobile or cell phones, are wireless **telephones** that **transmit** and receive messages via **radio signals.** They enable people to communicate over a wide area through a network of radio **antennas** and other equipment.

The American Telephone & Telegraph Company (commonly called AT&T) considered the development of a cellular telephone as early as 1915. Early versions of wireless phones were developed in the decades that followed. In 1979, Japan introduced the world's first commercial cellular telephone system. The first commercial cellular system in the United States went into operation in 1983.

Networks of radio antennas connect cell phone users around the world.

Early wireless phones were large, expensive, and unreliable. At first, not many people used them. But as technology advanced, the phones became smaller and cheaper, and their performance improved. Over time, the popularity of cell phones has risen dramatically. Wireless technology has begun to replace traditional wired service in many areas.

Most popular cell phones today are small enough to keep in a pocket. Many are equipped with additional features. For example, most cell phones can store phone numbers, calendar events, and other information. Many people use them to send text messages to friends or to play games. Some cell phones, called **smartphones,** have many of the same features as handheld computers. (For more information, see The Smartphone, pages 42-43).

Cell phones come in a variety of shapes and colors to fit each person's taste.

▶ Digital Television

After the late 1940's, **television** took on an increasingly important role in people's daily lives. However, television's pictures and sounds were often poor in quality, due to the limitations of early TV equipment and techniques. Over the years, a number of technological advances have changed the way that people experience television.

At first, all TV programs were in black and white. Color **broadcasts** first became available in 1953. Most early TV programs were broadcast live, and others were made from film, which required time to develop. The videotaping of programs began in the mid-1950's. **Videotape,** which does not need to be developed like film, enabled programs to be played back immediately after taping. Videotape also produced better-quality pictures and sounds.

In television's early days, most screens measured 7 or 10 inches (18 or 25 centimeters) diagonally. Today, 27-inch (69-centimeter) screens are common, and some televisions have screens as large as 60 inches (152 centimeters). Other TV sets have screens measuring only 3 inches (7.6 centimeters) and are small enough to fit in a pocket.

Digital television represents one of the biggest changes in television since the introduction of color. Digital systems convert television signals into the same numerical code used by computers. These systems provide stronger and more reliable signals, and they can fit more **channels** into the same signal space. They also allow for interactive programming

Televisions have changed, along with clothing fashions and furniture styles, since the 1950's.

and different language selections. In 2006, a new United States law required all major U.S. television stations to broadcast only in a digital format after February 17, 2009.

High-definition television (HDTV) is a type of digital television that produces extremely sharp images. It provides a picture approximately four times as sharp as standard television does. Major U.S. broadcasters started **broadcasting** digital television signals using HDTV in 1998.

F
U
N

F
A
C
T
The first remote control for televisions was developed in the 1950's. Called the "Lazy Bones," it was connected to the television by a wire. The wireless television remote control as we know it today was not developed until the 1970's.

Digital televisions keep getting larger but thinner.

▶ The Smartphone

With recent advances in wireless technology, more people own a **cellular telephone,** or cell phone, than ever before. The first cell phones were large and expensive. They were not very reliable, and they were incapable of doing anything more than making or receiving a call. All of this has changed.

At first, the main changes involved size. The phones gradually became smaller and smaller. Later, phones began to add more and more functions. In the early 2000's, devices called **smartphones** began to appear.

Smartphones have many of the same capabilities and features as handheld computers. In addition to storing phone numbers, addresses, and calendar information, smartphones can send and receive **e-mail** and even use the **Internet**. Smartphones may also include such features as digital cameras, digital music players, **electronic** games, and receivers for **Global Positioning Sys-**

Smartphones, like this one, are used for much more than just talking.

tem (GPS) navigation.

Many smartphones have features like a miniature keyboard, similar to that of a **typewriter.** Others have a **touch screen**. With a touch screen, the user can enter information by

Touch-screen technology was first developed in the 1970's. Today, touch screens have many uses. They are used by many stores and restaurants to process orders. They are also used for public information displays, like information centers at bookstores and directories in highrise office buildings.

pressing on parts of the device's screen. Some touch screens work with a penlike tool called a stylus. With some devices, the user can write or print on the screen with the stylus. Handwriting-recognition programs convert the written words to computer code.

Smartphones can perform many of the same functions as a full-sized **personal computer.** People can access information on the **World Wide Web** and communicate through voice, text, or images, no matter where they are.

A stylus is a tool that people can use with smartphones to write or to browse.

Important Dates in Communication

c. 3500 B.C. The Sumerians developed the first known writing system.

c. 3000 B.C. The Egyptians developed hieroglyphics.

c. 300 B.C. The Chinese started making paper.

c. A.D. 700 Block printing was practiced by the Chinese, Japanese, and Koreans.

c. 1045 Movable type is invented in China.

Mid-1400's The German inventor Johannes Gutenberg developed the printing press.

1840 The American painter and inventor Samuel F. B. Morse patented his electric telegraph.

1866 The first successful transatlantic telegraph cable linked Europe and North America.

1876 Alexander Graham Bell, a Scottish-born inventor, patented a type of telephone.

1895 The Italian inventor Guglielmo Marconi sent radio signals more than a mile through the air in the form of telegraph code signals.

1906 Reginald Fessenden, a Canadian-born physicist, transmitted voice by radio.

1929 Vladimir Zworykin, a Russian-born American scientist, demonstrated the first completely electronic television system.

1936 The British Broadcasting Corporation (BBC) accomplished the world's first TV broadcasts.

Mid-1950's Color television broadcasts became available.

1958 The United States launched the first communications satellite.

1960 Echo 1 became the first artificial satellite to receive radio signals from a ground station and reflect them back to Earth.

Late 1960's The Internet was developed in the United States.

Early 1980's Several companies began to market cellular telephones.

1980's Fax machines became widely popular in business.

1991 The arrival of the World Wide Web helped make the Internet popular and easier to use.

Late 1990's Digital television was developed to provide stronger and more reliable signals.

Early 2000's Smartphones become widely available.

▶ Glossary

alphabet a series of letters, each standing for particular sounds, used in a written language.

antenna a device that helps information pass from a transmitting location to a receiving location.

artificial satellite a manufactured object that continuously orbits Earth or some other body in space.

block printing a printing method in which a person uses a thin block of wood or other material to reproduce an image.

broadcast (n.) something sent out by radio or television; a radio or television program of speech, music, or the like; (v.) to send out programs by radio or television.

broadcasting the act of sending out programs by radio or television.

cellular telephone a wireless telephone that transmits and receives messages via radio signals.

channel a narrow band of electronic frequencies that carries the programs of a television or radio station.

citizens band a radio transmitting channel provided by the U.S. federal government for use by private citizens.

consonant any letter in the alphabet that is not a vowel.

digital television a system that converts television signals into the same numerical code used by computers.

electric current the movement or flow of electric charges.

electromagnet a temporary magnet formed when electric current flows through a wire or other conductor.

electromagnetic waves related patterns of electric and magnetic force that travel through space.

electronic of or having to do with electrons.

e-mail a message sent from one computer to another over a computer network.

etch to engrave (a design) on metal, glass, wood, mineral, or plastic by acid or heat that burns lines into it.

fax machine an electronic device that sends and receives written words and pictures over telephone lines.

Global Positioning System a worldwide navigation system that uses radio signals broadcast by satellites.

hieroglyphics a form of writing in which picture symbols represent ideas and sounds.

high-definition television a type of digital television that produces extremely sharp images.

Industrial Revolution a period in the late 1700's and early 1800's when the development of industries brought great change to many parts of the world.

instant messaging (IM) a feature that allows a computer user to see messages immediately as they are being typed by another user.

Internet a vast network of computers that connects many of the world's businesses, institutions, and individuals.

Linotype a machine used to arrange metal type for printing.

legend a type of folk story, generally based on real people or events.

lithography a printing technique involving grease-based designs on flat surfaces. It works because grease and water do not mix.

mass communication any form of communication (such as the press, radio, or television) that reaches large numbers of people.

Middle Ages the period in European history between ancient and modern times, from about the A.D. 400's through the 1400's.

mill a building where manufacturing is done.

movable type a system for printing in which separate pieces of metal type are used for each character to be printed.

myth a type of folk story, usually involving religious subjects or events from long ago.

papyrus a water plant from which paper was made.

patent (n.) a government-issued document that grants an inventor exclusive rights to an invention for a limited time; (v.) to get a patent for.

personal computer a computer used by one person at a time.

photocomposition any method of assembling types and illustrations on photographic paper or film, or on a printing plate.

printing press a machine for printing from types, plates, or blocks.

radio signal information that travels through air and space as radio waves.

Renaissance a period of great revival of art and learning in Europe during the 1300's, 1400's, and 1500's.

Roman of or having to do with ancient Rome or its people. The Roman Empire controlled most of Europe and the Middle East from 27 B.C. to 476 A.D.

satellite see **artificial satellite.**

search engine a computer program used to find information stored on computers.

smartphone a device that combines the features of a cellular telephone and handheld computer.

syllable a word or part of a word pronounced as a unit.

telegram a message sent by telegraph.

telegraph an instrument used to send messages by means of wires and electric current.

telephone an instrument that sends and receives voice messages in the form of electrical or radio signals.

touch screen an electronic display screen on which the user selects options by touching the screen.

television the process of sending pictures of an object, scene, or event through the air or over wires by means of electricity so that people in many places can see them at once.

transmit to send out (signals, voices, music, or pictures) by means of radio or television or by wire.

transmitter a part of a radio or television broadcasting system that sends out signals.

typesetting the act, art, or process of setting type for printing.

typewriter a machine that produces printed letters and figures on paper.

videotape a wide magnetized tape with tracks for recording and reproducing both sound and picture.

vowel a letter that stands for speech sounds produced by not blocking the breath with the lips, teeth, or tongue, generally with the vocal cords vibrating.

walkie-talkie a two-way radio that provides quick voice communication over short distances.

World Wide Web a vast system of computer files (including text, illustrations, sounds, and moving pictures) linked together on the Internet.

X rays invisible rays that can be used to produce pictures of bones and other body structures.

Additional Resources

Books:

- *Alexander Graham Bell and the Telephone: The Invention that Changed Communication* by Samuel Willard Crompton (Chelsea House Publishers, 2009).

- *Amazing Leonardo da Vinci Inventions You Can Build Yourself* by Maxine Anderson (Nomad Press VT, 2006).

- *Did You Hear the News?: History of Communication* by Allison Lassieur (Raintree, 2007).

- *Great Inventions: The Illustrated Science Encyclopedia* by Peter Harrison, Chris Oxlade, and Stephen Bennington (Southwater Publishing, 2001).

- *Great Inventions of the 20th Century* by Peter Jedicke (Chelsea House Publications, 2007).

- *The History of the Telephone* by Elizabeth Raum (Heinemann Library, 2008).

- *How to Enter and Win an Invention Contest* by Edwin J. Sobey (Enslow, 1999).

- *Inventions* by Valerie Wyatt (Kids Can Press, 2003).

- *Leonardo, Beautiful Dreamer* by Robert Byrd (Dutton, 2003).

- *Samuel Morse and the Story of the Telegraph* by Susan Zannos (Mitchell Lane, 2005).

- *So You Want to Be an Inventor?* By Judith St. George (Philomel Books, 2002).

- *What a Great Idea! Inventions that Changed the World* by Stephen M. Tomecek (Scholastic, 2003).

Web Sites:

- Victorian Technology
  http://www.bbc.co.uk/history/british/victorians/victorian_technology_04.shtml
  This Web page, maintained by the British Broadcasting Company (BBC), explores how advances in transportation and communication transformed Great Britain during the Victorian age.

- FCC's History of Communications
  http://www.fcc.gov/omd/history
  This section of the U.S. Federal Communications Commission's Web site discusses the history of communication in the United States.

- Franklin Institute's History of Communications
  http://www.fi.edu/learn/case-files/communication.html
  Includes a brief history of communication, as well as links to biographies of important scientists in communication.

- Guglielmo Marconi
  http://www.invent.org/hall_of_fame/97.html
  Information about Guglielmo Marconi and the radio from the National Inventors Hall of Fame.

- National Inventors Hall of Fame
  http://www.invent.org/index.asp
  Information on inventions and inventors from the National Inventors Hall of Fame.

- American Experience: The Telephone
  http://www.pbs.org/wgbh/amex/telephone/index.html
  A Web site maintained by the U.S. Public Broadcasting Service (PBS) that includes information relating to the invention of the telephone.

▶ Index